THE BROCKHAMPTON LIBRARY

guide to
Astrology

BROCKHAMPTON PRESS
LONDON

© 1996 Geddes & Grosset Ltd, David Dale House,
New Lanark ML11 9DJ

This edition published 1996 by Brockhampton Press, a member of
Hodder Headline PLC Group

All rights reserved. No part of this publication may be reproduced,
stored in a retrieval system, or transmitted, in any form or by any
means, electronic, mechanical, photocopying, recording or
otherwise, without the prior permission of the copyright holder.

ISBN 1 86019 252 1

Printed and bound in the UK

Contents

History   5

The Solar System   10
  The Planets   10

A Few Technicalities   14
  The Great Year   20
  Signs and Symbols   21

The Signs of the Zodiac   24
  Aries   24
  Taurus   25
  Gemini   25
  Cancer   25
  Leo   26
  Virgo   26
  Libra   26
  Scorpio   26
  Sagittarius   27
  Capricorn   27
  Aquarius   27
  Pisces   28

Groups of the Zodiac and Rulings   29
  Influence of the planets   33
  The ruling planets and relationships   34

The Houses of the Chart   35
  The Houses   37
  The First House   37
  The Second House   37

The Third House	37
The Fourth House	38
The Fifth House	38
The Sixth House	39
The Seventh House	39
The Eighth House	39
The Ninth House	40
The Tenth House	40
The Eleventh House	40
The Twelfth House	41

The Sun Signs   42

The Chart   62

History

Astrology is an ancient craft that has its origin in the mists of time. It is impossible to place accurately the beginnings but one thing that is certain is that astrology began as a subject intimately combined with astronomy. Its history is therefore the history of astronomy until the two subjects parted company, a split that essentially began when Nicolai Copernicus (1473–1543) published his book *De revolutionibus*. In this book he postulated that contrary to earlier thinking, in which the Earth was the centre of the solar system, the Sun actually formed the focus about which all the planets orbited.

It is thought that there was some study of these subjects five to six thousand years ago when Chaldean priests made maps of the skies. The Chaldeans were the most ancient Babylonians. It was believed that heavenly bodies exerted influence upon man and whatever could not be ascribed to man, must be due to actions of the gods, or the deities of the planets. Subsequent study of the solar system began as purely observation because records and other data for calculation simply did not exist. The Egyptian and Greek civilizations gave much to the theories and practice of astrology although much remained unwritten. It is said that the Chaldeans instructed the priests of the Pharaohs in astrology, and monuments exist that show a working knowledge of the subject. This was around 400–350 BC. A little earlier, in Greece around the beginning of the sixth century BC, the philosopher Thales (*c.*643–*c.*546 BC) studied astronomy/astrology as did Pythagoras (569–470 BC) who was credited by Copernicus as the person who developed the theory that the Earth and other planets revolved around the Sun.

There were many other Greek students, notably: Plato; Hippocrates, who combined astrology with medical diagnosis; Hipparchus, the founder of observational astronomy, who in 134 BC discovered a new star; and Claudius Ptolemaeus (100–178 AD). Ptolemy wrote the *Almagest*, which is a star catalogue of just over a thousand stars, and also a consideration of the motion of the Moon and the planets. He also wrote the *Tetrabiblos*, the earliest surviving book on astrology.

In Rome and the extended empire at this time, astrology was held in very high regard, and great faith was placed in the work and advice of astrologers who were appointed to the Emperors. The Moon was considered particularly influential and can be found depicted on many of their coins. Among the many Romans active in this field were Porphyry (232–304 AD), who is said to have developed the house method, and Julius Maternus (around 300 AD), who wrote a number of books on astrology.

From about 500 AD Arabs became the prime movers in science and philosophy, but by the early Middle Ages (the thirteenth century) interest was rekindled in Europe, at which time astrology had been divided into three distinct fields: *natural* or *mundane* astrology, which is prominent in forecasting national events, weather, etc; *horary* astrology, used to answer a question through the use of a chart drawn up for the actual time of asking; and *judicial* astrology, in which the fortune of an individual is determined by using a birth chart.

The fifteenth and sixteenth centuries in Europe saw the rise of several famous names, including the Polish astronomer Copernicus. Although Copernicus concurred with the views of Pythagoras, he could not prove the theory, and many attribute the real establishment of the principle (i.e. that the planets orbit the Sun) to Johann Kepler (1571–1630), the German astronomer. The medieval precursor of chemistry was alchemy, and one famous practitioner was Phillipus Aureolus Paracelsus (1493–1541), who also had some astrological leanings. He believed that the Sun, planets and stars influenced people, whether for good or evil. From this era also came Nostradamus (1503–1566). Michael Nostradamus has become one of the most famous of astrologists and prophets, and he also studied medicine. Almost from the outset it was thought that medical knowledge must, by necessity, include an understanding of astrology.

The work of the Dane Tycho Brahe (1546–1601) could, in some respects, be considered a watershed in the study of astrology/astronomy. Brahe became an observer of the heavens and in so doing was recognized as the most accurate since Hipparchus, centuries before. He prepared tables, designed instruments and studied the motion of the planets, particularly Mars, and it was this initial work that led Kepler to formulate his famous laws of planetary motion. Kepler was assistant to Brahe when the latter moved to Prague following the death of his patron, King Frederick. Kepler's work proved to be pivotal in advancing the understanding of astronomy. Kepler compared the work of Ptolemy, Copernicus and Tycho Brahe to produce three laws:

1. The orbit of each planet is an ellipse with the Sun at one of the foci (an ellipse has two foci.)
2. A line drawn from a planet to the Sun sweeps out equal areas in equal times.
3. The squares of the sidereal periods (time taken to orbit the Sun, measured relative to the stars) are proportional to the cubes of the mean distances from the Sun.

Kepler believed that the stars exerted an influence upon events and that astrology could predict the most mundane of happenings. During the sixteenth and seventeenth centuries there were many famous names who combined astrology with astronomy, mathematics or, commonly, medicine. These included the Italian physicist Galileo Galilei, a French professor of mathematics and doctor of medicine, Jean Morin, an Italian monk and mathematician, Placidus de Tito, and in England, William Lilly, who became famous as a practitioner of horary astrology and accurately predicted the Great Fire of London in 1666.

The poet John Dryden used astrology in predicting numerous events in his own life and the lives of his sons, including both their deaths. Following Dryden's own death in 1700, although not because of it, astrological practice declined on the continent but flourished in England. This influence extended to France at the start of the nineteenth century, where a sound scientific basis to the subject was sought.

William Allan (1800–1917), otherwise known as Alan Leo, was considered by many to be the father of modern astrology. He lectured widely throughout England and edited a magazine called *Modern Astrology*. He was also a professional astrologer and a prolific author on the subject, writing 30 books. In 1915 he founded the Astrological Lodge of London. Although the war years were disruptive to the study and practice of astrology, a large following was developed in North America. However, continental Europe suffered during the Second World War as Hitler's forces caused wholesale destruction, and Hitler himself, unhappy with adverse astrological predictions, destroyed books and records and incarcerated unfortunate practitioners.

Today astrology holds interest for many people, and growing numbers are becoming fascinated by its study. However, there is a dichotomy between astrology and astronomy.

The Solar System

The early visualizations of the heavens and the stars showed the Earth at the centre of a large revolving sphere. It was thought that the stars seen in the sky were somehow fastened onto the inner surface of this sphere. The stars that appeared to revolve around the Earth but did not move in relation to each other were called the 'fixed stars'. Among the many fixed stars there are some in particular that have certain characteristics and that can be used in astrological charts. For example, Regulus (or Alpha Leonis) is the brightest star in the constellation of Leo and signifies pride, good luck and success.

From early times it was noted that while many stars remained fixed, five in particular did not, and these wandered about the sky. These were the planets of the solar system because at that time not all eight remaining planets (other than Earth) had been identified. The discovery of Uranus, Neptune and Pluto followed the invention of the telescope, and Uranus was the first planet so observed, in 1781.

For the purposes of astrology, the Sun, which is actually a star, is considered as a planet. It is approximately 150 million kilometres from Earth and has a diameter of 1.4 million kilometres. Energy is generated in the core, from nuclear fusion, where the temperature is about fifteen million degrees.

The Planets

The Moon is a satellite of Earth but for convenience is also treated as a planet. It orbits the Earth roughly every 27 days, and the same face is always kept towards Earth, lit by light reflected from the Sun. The Moon seems to change size—

the process known as waxing and waning—and it is called 'new' when it is situated between the Earth and the Sun and, because it is not illuminated, cannot be seen. The full Moon occurs about 14 days later, when the full face is totally illuminated.

Planets with their orbits between the Sun and the Earth's orbit are called 'inferior'. There are two planets in this category, Mercury and Venus. Mercury is the smallest planet in the solar system and takes 88 Earth days to complete one orbit, rotating slowly on its axis, and taking 58 Earth days for one revolution. Its elliptical orbit is eccentric, varying in distance from the Sun from 47 to 70 million kilometres.

Venus is the brightest planet seen from Earth and is known as the morning or evening star. It is about 108 million kilometres from the Sun and has a diameter similar to Earth's, at 12,300 kilometres. Venus spins very slowly on its axis, and a day is equivalent to 24.3 Earth days, and a year is 225 days. It is unusual in being the only planet to revolve in the opposite direction to the path of its orbit.

The remaining planets, from Mars to Pluto, are called the 'superior planets', being on the distant side of Earth from the Sun. Mars takes about 687 Earth days to complete an orbit, and a day is just a fraction longer than one Earth day. The surface is solid and mainly red in colour because of the type of rock. There are many surface features, some of which are attributed to the action of water, although none is found there now. Mars is sometimes a dominant feature of the night sky, particularly when it occasionally approaches nearer to Earth, and it has from ancient times exerted considerable fascination.

Jupiter is the largest and heaviest planet in the solar system and has a diameter of 142,800 kilometres. The planet gives out more energy than it receives from the Sun and must therefore have an internal energy source. It is due, in part, to this that the atmosphere is seen to be in steady movement. Parallel bands of colour are seen, but a particularly noticeable feature is the Great Red Spot, which is thought to be an enormous storm, larger than Earth, coloured red because of the presence of phosphorus. The magnetic field of Jupiter is thousands of times stronger than Earth's, and radio waves emanate from the planet. Jupiter has 18 satellites, or moons, of which four called the 'Galilean satellites'—Io, Europa, Ganymede and Callisto—because they were first seen by Galileo in 1610. There are three other groups of satellites, of which the innermost contains Adastrea, Amalthea, Metis and Thebe.

The next planet out from the Sun is Saturn, the second largest in the solar system. It has a diameter of 120,800 kilometres and the orbit takes 29 Earth years at a distance of 1507 million kilometres from the Sun. Because of its rapid rotation, Saturn is flattened at the poles with a consequent bulging at its equator. A day lasts for a little over 10 hours, and the surface temperature is 170 degrees. The most obvious and interesting feature of Saturn is its rings, which consist of ice, dust and rock debris, and some of which may have derived from the break-up of a satellite. The rings are about a quarter of a million kilometres across, and there are three main ones but hundreds of smaller ones.

Saturn also has 24 satellites, or moons, of which Titan is the largest with a diameter of 5200 kilometres (larger than Mercury). Some moons were discovered by the Voyager spacecraft in 1989, including Atlas, Calypso and Prometheus.

The planets Mercury through to Saturn were all known to astrologers and astronomers for many years. The remaining planets, Uranus, Neptune and Pluto, were discovered only in modern times, after the advent of the telescope. These are therefore often called the 'modern planets' by astrologers.

Uranus is 50,080 kilometres in diameter and a day lasts 17 hours while a year is equivalent to 84 Earth years. Because of its tilted axis, some parts of the planet's surface are in light for about 40 years and then in darkness for the remainder of its year. Uranus was discovered by William Herschel in 1781 but was something of a mystery until 1986 and the approach of Voyager. It has a faint ring system and 15 moons, some of which are very small indeed (less than 50 kilometres in diameter).

Neptune was discovered in 1846, but its existence was earlier correctly postulated because of observed irregularities in the orbit of Uranus. It takes 165 Earth years to complete an orbit and is almost 4.5 billion kilometres from the Sun. It is 17 times the mass of Earth and has a diameter at its equator of 48,600 kilometres. There are three rings and eight known satellites, the largest of which, Titan, is similar in size to the Earth's Moon.

Pluto, the smallest and most distant planet from the Sun, had its existence predicted because of its effect on the orbits of Neptune and Uranus and was finally discovered in 1930, although little is known about it. A day is equivalent to almost seven days on Earth, and a year is nearly 249 Earth years. Pluto has a very wide elliptical orbit, which brings it closest to the Sun (its *perihelion*) once in each orbit. Because of its great distance from the Sun (7.4 billion kilometres at its maximum), the surface temperature is very low, about 230 degrees. In 1979, one small moon, called Charon, was discovered, but since it is about one quarter the size of Pluto itself, the two act almost as a double planet system.

A Few Technicalities

As has been mentioned, the orbits of the planets are elliptical rather than circular, and there is a degree of eccentricity as well. When viewed from Earth, this combination of factors produces what may appear to be peculiar effects, for example, planets may move around the sky, slow and then appear to move backwards for a time. This apparent backward motion is called *retrograde* and is simply due to the Earth moving more quickly through its orbit in comparison to another planet. It *seems* as though the planet being observed is moving backwards, but in reality it is moving forwards, albeit in the line of sight at a slower rate. It is similar to a fast train moving alongside a slow train, which makes the latter appear to be moving backwards. In astronomical tables R denotes retrograde while D marks a return to direct motion.

Another astronomical parameter used in astrology is that of conjunctions. A *conjunction* is when two or more planets (including the Sun of course) are in a line when viewed from Earth. On occasion, Earth, Venus and the Sun will all be in a straight line. If Venus is between Earth and the Sun it is called an 'inferior conjunction'. If, however, Venus is on the other side of the Sun from Earth, it is a 'superior conjunction'. The same applies to Mercury. *Opposition* is when, for example, Earth lies between the Sun and Mars; then Mars is in opposition. Opposition is when one of the superior planets (all except Mercury, Venus and, of course, Earth) is opposite

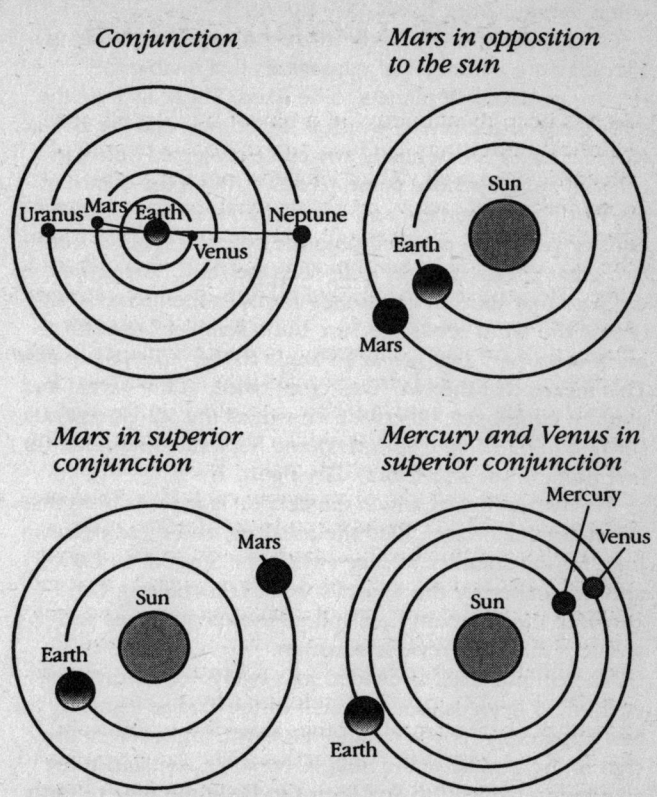

Figure 1: Conjunctions

the Sun in the sky, i.e. making an angle of 180 degrees when viewed from Earth. [*See* figure 1].

Of vital significance to the correct interpretive study of astrology are a number of parameters that enable the relative positions of planets to be fixed. These include the three great circles, one of which is the ecliptic, and the Zodiac. (A great circle is essentially any circle projected onto the celestial sphere whose plane passes through the centre of the Earth.) The horizon and celestial equator (the Earth's equator projected outward onto the celestial sphere) form two great circles, and the ecliptic is the third. The *ecliptic* is the path that the Sun apparently forms in the heavens. Of course the Earth orbits the Sun, but it seems from Earth to mark out a path that lies at an angle to the celestial equator. This means that the two lines cross twice, at the vernal and autumn equinoxes, otherwise known as the March equinox (or first point of the sign Aries) and September equinox (or first point of the sign Libra). [*See* figure 2]

The two points at which the ecliptic is farthest from the celestial equator are called the solstices, and these occur in June for the summer solstice (when the Sun enters Cancer) and December for the winter solstice (on entering Capricorn). In the southern hemisphere these equinoxes and solstices mark the reverse situation.

The ecliptic itself is divided into twelve equal divisions, each of 30 degrees, one for each of the Zodiac signs. As the Sun apparently moves around the Earth, it goes from one sign of the Zodiac to the next. A person's Sun sign is the sign before which the Sun seems to be at the time of birth.

The *Zodiac* is a 'band' in the heavens that extends to seven or eight degrees on either side of the ecliptic. Within this band, or path, are contained the apparent movements

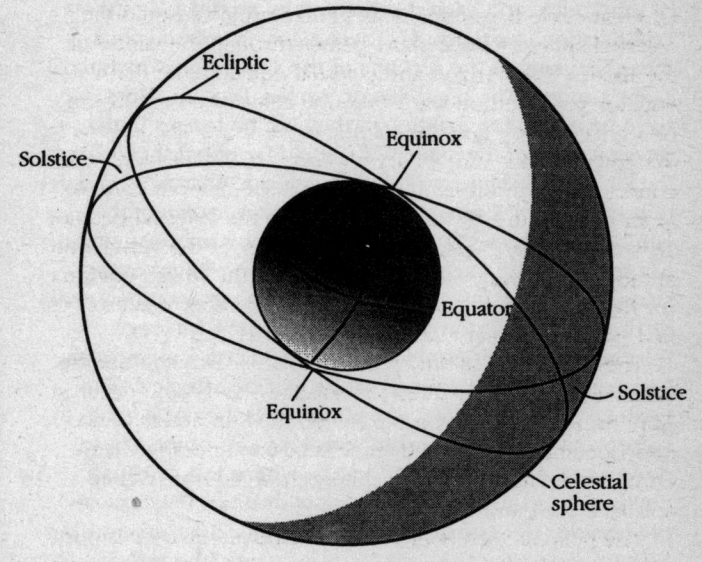

Figure 2: The ecliptic and the celestial sphere

of the planets, except Pluto. The solar system can be considered as a relatively planar feature, and within this plane the Earth revolves around the Sun. The planes of the orbits of all the other planets are within seven degrees of Earth's, save for Pluto, which is nearer 17 degrees. The Zodiac is then split into twelve segments of 30 degrees, one for each sign of the Zodiac and each represented by a particular star constellation [see figure 3]. These signs are essentially a means of naming the sections of the sky within which the planets move. The constellation names, Scorpio, Libra, etc, have no significance although they are bound up in the development of the subject. It should be noted that today, the 30-degree segments no longer coincide with the constellation because of a phenomenon called *precession of the equinoxes*. Precession results in the Earth's axis of rotation not remaining in the same position but forming a cone shape traced out in space. It is due to the gravitational pulls of the Sun and Moon producing a turning force, or torque. This occurs only because the Earth bulges at the equator—a perfect sphere would not be affected. The Earth takes almost 26,000 years (known as the Great Year) to sweep out the cone, and in astrology the point Aries 0 degrees (the First Point of Aries), where the celestial equator cuts the ecliptic, moves with time. Because of precession, the equator crossing-point moves around the ecliptic, and now the First Point of Aries (the vernal equinox of astronomy) lies in the constellation of Pisces and is soon to move into Aquarius. The 30 degrees along the ecliptic that is Aries remains the 30 degrees counted from the vernal equinox, although that equinox is farther back each year (this is, therefore, retrograde motion). Aries has been considered the first sign from hundreds of

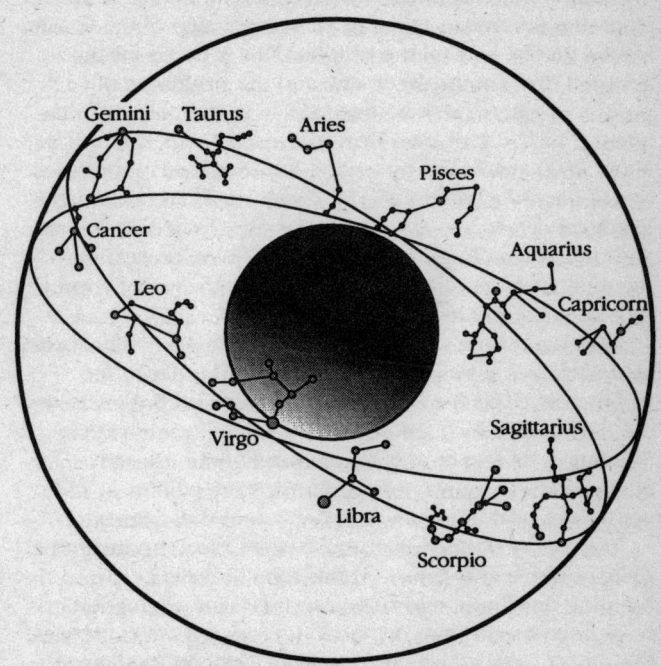

Figure 3: The Constellations

years BC, when it was believed that the Earth had a birthday.

The Great Year

The Great Year, as mentioned, is divided into twelve periods when the equinox is taken to be against each of the constellations that lie around the ecliptic. This is by no means an accurate division or placement, and the beginning of each period, or age, cannot be fixed easily as the constellations overlap and vary in size. However, each age is taken to be about 2000 years, and by tracing the characteristics of each age in history a pattern can be constructed. From available historical details, the last 2000 years are typified as Piscean and before that Taurean. This links with the precession of the equinoxes mentioned earlier, and so the next period will be the *Age of Aquarius*.

Each age of the Great Year identified this far has certain characteristics associated with the sign. The *Age of Leo* began about 10000 BC and has as its animal representative the lion, with which are connected creativity and regality. The Sun is its planet. It is interesting to note the early attempts at art, by way of prehistoric cave paintings, and of course the vital importance of the Sun in those times.

The *Age of Cancer* (8000–6000 BC) is associated with the traits of home and family. At this time humans began building dwellings, and some carvings symbolizing fertility have been found from this period. From 6000–4000 BC was the *Age of Gemini*, which represents a sign of intellectual capacity. It is thought that writing began in some form during this Age, hence communication, a further characteristic of Gemini, became important. Civilization developed apace with cuneiform writing by the end of the Age, and the distinct possibility that humans had begun to travel and explore. The *Age of Taurus* followed, from 4000–2000 BC, and there are numerous instances that relate to the Taurean features of solidity and security with beauty. These traits are seen in the Egyptian dynasties and the worship of the bull, and in the enormous and ornate temples and the pyramids. The next age is that of *Aries* (2000 BC–0 AD). Aggressive and assertive qualities are associated with Aries, as are physical fitness and supremacy. These are balanced by courage and also harmony. All these characteristics are well exemplified by the Greeks, who dominated in battle and architecture and yet created the first democratic government. The symbol of the ram found an outlet in numerous ways, including as an emblem of the Roman army.

We are currently in the *Age of Pisces* (0–2000 AD), albeit towards the end of the period. It began with the birth of Christ, and there are numerous connections to the sign of the fish at this time. The secret symbol for the early Christians was the fish, Jesus was called *Ichthus*, the fish, and many of his disciples were fishermen. Qualities such as kindness, charity and forgiveness are typical, as is selflessness, although an element of confusion can also be discerned. We are on the brink of the new Age, that of *Aquarius* (2000–4000 AD), but in many respects the signs are already there to be seen. Aquarian influence can be seen in the strong presence of science and technology and space travel. Also Aquarian, is a sense of detachment and of being impersonal.

Signs and Symbols

Each sign of the Zodiac has a particular graphical representation, called a glyph, which itself relates to an animal or something similar. The same applies to the planets, and these symbols are used extensively, with others, in constructing an astrological chart. The Zodiac sign and symbols are as follows:

Symbol/Sign	Representation	Name
♈ Aries	the ram's horns	The Ram
♉ Taurus	the bull's head	The Bull
♊ Gemini	two children	The Twins
♋ Cancer	breasts	The Crab
♌ Leo	the heart, or the lion's tail	The Lion
♍ Virgo	the female genitalia	The Virgin
♎ Libra	a pair of scales	The Balance
♏ Scorpio	the male genitalia	The Scorpion
♐ Sagittarius	the Centaur's arrow	The Archer
♑ Capricorn	a goat's head and fish's tail	The Goat
♒ Aquarius	waves of water or air	The Waterbearer
♓ Pisces	two fish	The Fishes

The glyphs of the planets are as follows:

Planet	Symbol
Sun	☉
Moon	☽
Mercury	☿
Venus	♀
Mars	♂
Jupiter	♃
Saturn	♄

Planet	*Symbol*
Uranus	♅
Neptune	♆
Pluto	♇

These planetary symbols are all made up of essentially the same elements, the cross, the half-circle, and the circle, all in different combinations. These pictorial representations are linked with the very early days of human beings, when communication was achieved using such graphical methods. As such, these elements each have a particular significance:

The circle represents eternity, something without end, the spirit; a circle with a dot inside signifies that the spirit or power is beginning to come out; the cross represents the material world; and the semicircle stands for the soul

The Signs of the Zodiac

The signs appear to have got their names from the depths of history and prehistory, and do not necessarily concur with their astronomical counterparts, the constellations. In some civilizations, the signs were attributed to parts of the body. The likeliest race to have adopted this were the Greeks, who also linked the signs to various plants.

Aries	–	the head
Libra	–	the kidneys
Taurus	–	throat
Scorpio	–	genitalia
Gemini	–	hands and arms
Sagittarius	–	hips and thighs
Cancer	–	the breasts
Capricorn	–	the knee
Leo	–	the heart
Aquarius	–	calf and ankle
Virgo	–	intestines
Pisces	–	the feet

Below are given the main features of the signs of the Zodiac, and these will be followed later by a fuller description of the character and personal details associated with the various sun signs, i.e. when the Sun passes through each of the signs as it appears to move on the ecliptic.

Aries
The astrological new year occurs around 21 March, when the

Sun enters Aries, and this new aspect is mirrored in typical Arian traits of energy, keenness and enthusiasm. The Arian can be something of a pioneer and thus somewhat self-centred with a selfish streak. Aries is the most personal of the signs.

Taurus

Taureans seek and reflect stability, security, and are generally practical with a possessive side to their character. Risks will be taken only if they are absolutely essential, and even then it will be only after a great deal of careful thought. In general Taureans are trustworthy and pleasant and yet unenterprising, which in some may lead to them become a little boring.

Gemini

This third sign of the Zodiac is that of the heavenly twins, which, not surprisingly, can surface as a certain duality, which in a negative sense may result in someone being two-faced. Geminians are intelligent, quick of mind, versatile, and are often good communicators. If the dual nature is too strongly negative then it may lead to a lack of achievement through being over-committed and trying to do too many things at once.

Cancer

Changeable, sympathetic, kind, hard on the outside but easily hurt or offended, emotional and devoted—a home and family builder. These are all Cancerian traits and paint an essentially sensitive picture but with the strengths of devotion and faithfulness. Intellectually, Cancerians are very intuitive and have a strong imagination. If these traits are over-stressed or misused, it can lead to restlessness and over-worry.

Leo

Leo is the only sign ruled by the Sun and, like the lion, so-called king of the beasts, the Leonian can be regal, dignified and magnanimous. They are faithful, trusting but strong-willed, with fixed principles and ideas, and yet if carried too far this may result in bossiness. Similarly, someone may become snobbish, conceited and domineering.

Virgo

Virgoans are typically the worker type; they dislike a leading role in anything, and yet they are intellectually very capable though with a tendency to worry. In work and at home they pay attention to detail with precision and clarity. Closeness to others may be avoided, resulting in the perception among others of Virgoans keeping to themselves, which in turn may be misinterpreted as inhospitality.

Libra

This seventh sign of the Zodiac is opposite to Aries, which makes Librans interested in relating to a partner. As such they tend to be companionable, tactful and like to be in pleasant surroundings. Librans are often unfairly dubbed as lazy. They may also have a tendency to be quite aggressive. A Libran may be of the type who sits on the fence over an issue and, seeing both sides of an argument, may be impossibly indecisive.

Scorpio

This sign is one of intense energy, with deep, passionate feelings about the object of their attention, be it a person or an issue. Scorpios can be passionate, but in excess this can result in resentment, jealousy and even hatred. However, they can equally be warm and charming, and their virtues become apparent when dealing with real life rather than more trivial matters.

Sagittarius
In the earlier days of astrology, Sagittarius was always represented by a man joined to a horse, signifying the duality of the sign—a combination of strength and intelligence. Sagittarians are often intellectuals with a thirst for a challenge and an ability of body and mind to match. Taken to extremes, these traits can mean restlessness, carelessness, extravagance and a tendency to 'horseplay'.

Capricorn
Capricornians tend to be practical, ambitious and caring, and they often possess an excellent sense of humour. In personal relationships caution is their watchword but once decided they will make good partners. Capricornians are also traditionalists and excel in routine work or in organizational capacities. On the negative side, they may become too mean and stern, and caution may turn into selfishness.

Aquarius
Aquarians are typically independent and individualistic, and also friendly. Indeed, friendships once formed tend to be faithful, although contact with others can be rather impersonal. The freedom required by an Aquarian makes them paradoxical when it comes to love. However, the enquiring mind and originality is seen to good effect in pursuit of art or working in science and technology. An excess of

Aquarian traits produces someone who is rebellious, tactless and eccentric.

Pisces

The last sign of the Zodiac, Pisces, is typified by a sensitivity that may border on the inhibited unless encouraged. Pisceans can be inspired and highly intuitive, although this may be clouded by mood swings, from elation to depression. Kindness is a common trait, and there is often a strong spiritual faith. In excess, Piscean characteristics may result in muddled thinking, weakness of character and excessive worry.

Groups of the Zodiac and Rulings

The twelve signs of the Zodiac are traditionally subdivided into a number of groups. The members of each group share certain characteristics that in terms of chart interpretation provide additional information rather than primary details.

The first grouping is the *triplicities*, otherwise known as the elements, and consists of the signs for fire, earth, air and water. Aries, Leo and Sagittarius are the *fire triplicity*. This sign is represented by a keenness and enthusiasm and a tendency literally to burn with excitement. Often more sensitive people will be considered slow and dealt with impatiently. While people with the fire sign may be lively and exuberant, their fault will often be that they are too lively. However, such tendencies are likely to be offset, to some extent, by features elsewhere in a chart.

The *earth triplicity* contains Taurus, Virgo and Capricorn and, as might be expected, people with this sign are 'down to earth', although the earth sign is not totally dominant. However, the beneficial aspects include practicality and caution, and although considered dull by livelier people, there is a reassuring solidity and trustworthiness about people with this sign.

Gemini, Libra and Aquarius form the *air triplicity*, and communication is one of the key attributes. An 'ideas person' would have this sign prominent in his or her chart, but a potential fault can be that schemes and ideas occupy too much time at the expense of productivity. In addition, such people can be dismissive of sensitivity or caution in others.

The final triplicity is that of *water*, and it contains Cancer, Scorpio and Pisces. Such people are naturally sensitive and intuitive, and often inspired, while also emotional and protective. Such people tend to be cautious of those with strong personalities, and their own faults may result from being too emotional.

It is often the case that people who have a shared strength in these signs will be compatible. Reference to the elements produces obvious attractions:

Fire	air fans the flames while water puts them out and earth smothers them.
Earth	water refreshes it while air and fire dry it out.
Air	fire responds to air, while earth and water restrict it.
Water	earth holds it, but air and fire diminish it.

The *quadruplicities* (otherwise known as qualities) form the second grouping. In this case the signs of the Zodiac are divided into three groups of four. The three qualities are 'cardinal', 'fixed' and 'mutable'. Aries, Libra, Cancer and Capricorn are of the *cardinal quadruplicity*. People with this sign dominant in their chart are outgoing and tend to lead. Taurus, Scorpio, Leo and Aquarius are of the *fixed quadruplicity*, which implies stability and a resistance to change. The *mutable quadruplicity* includes the remaining signs, Gemini, Sagittarius, Virgo and Pisces, and all have an adaptability. They often appear selfless.

The third grouping is into positive and negative (otherwise known as masculine and feminine). In essence these are descriptive rather than definitive terms and equate in a general sense to being self-expressive or extrovert (positive) on the one hand and receptive or introvert on the other. This does not mean that if a woman has a masculine sign she is not to be considered feminine, and vice versa.

Taking into account the three groupings, the Zodiac signs are as follows:

Aries	–	fire, cardinal, masculine
Taurus	–	earth, fixed, feminine
Gemini	–	air, mutable, masculine
Cancer	–	water, cardinal, feminine
Leo	–	fire, fixed, masculine
Virgo	–	earth, mutable, feminine
Libra	–	air, cardinal, masculine
Scorpio	–	water, fixed, feminine
Sagittarius	–	fire, mutable, masculine
Capricorn	–	earth, cardinal, feminine
Aquarius	–	air, fixed, masculine
Pisces	–	water, mutable, feminine

When interpreting charts, another useful link between signs is *polarity*. This is the relationship between a sign and the opposite sign across the Zodiac. Thus, on a circular display of the twelve signs, Aries is opposite Libra, Cancer opposite Capricorn, Taurus opposite Scorpio, etc. The signs thus opposed do not, however, have opposite tendencies; rather, the polar signs complement each other.

Before turning to the concept of ruling planets, it will be helpful to consider a few other definitions and some lines and angles that are critical in the construction of a chart.

The *ascendant* is defined as the degree of a sign (or the ecliptic) that is rising above the horizon at an individual's birth and marks the junction of the first sign. This is essentially the beginning for any astrological chart construction and interpretation, and after calculation is marked on the chart, working clockwise upwards from the horizon line, which runs east-west across the chart. The ascendant is very significant and can only be constructed if a birth time is known. The significance of the ascendant is that it indicates the beginning of the personality and how an individual faces the world—his or her true self. There are many other factors that may lessen the influence of the ascendant sign, but if some characteristic comes out of a chart that reinforces one linked to the ascendant, then it will be a very significant trait.

The *descendant* is the point opposite to the ascendant, at 180 degrees to it, and is always the cusp, or junction, of the seventh house. Although it may often be left out of charts, the descendant is meant to indicate the sort of partner, friends, etc, with whom one associates and feels comfortable.

The *midheaven* is often abbreviated to MC, from the Latin *medium coeli*. At the time when one particular sign of the Zodiac is appearing over the horizon (the ascendant) there will inevitably be another sign that is at its greatest height. This sign is then said to culminate at the upper meridian of the appropriate place—in brief, the midheaven is the intersection of the meridian [*see* figure 2] with the ecliptic at birth. The significance of the midheaven is that it relates to the career of an individual and the way in which it is pursued. It can also provide a general indication of aims and intentions and the type of partner that may be sought. The point opposite to the midheaven is the *imum coeli* and is connected to the subject's origins, his or her early and late life, and parental/domestic circumstances. The *imum coeli*, or IC, is sometimes referred to as the nadir, but strictly speaking this is incorrect. The nadir is actually a point in the heavens that is directly opposite the zenith, which itself is a point in the heavens directly over any place.

Influence of the planets

Every sign of the Zodiac has what is called a *ruling planet*, which is the planet that rules the ascendant sign. From the list below, it can be seen that if someone has Pisces rising, the ruling planet will be Neptune. Each planet rules one sign, save for Venus and Mercury, which each rule two. Of course, before William Herschel discovered Uranus in 1781 there were only seven planets (including the Sun and Moon) and therefore three further planets ruled two signs; Saturn ruled Aquarius in addition to Capricorn, Jupiter ruled Pisces in addition to Sagittarius, and Mars ruled Scorpio in addition to Aries.

There are also a number of planets that are termed personal. The *personal planets* are the Sun and Moon (which are always personal), the planet that rules the ascendant sign (called the chart ruler). The Sun ruler is the planet that rules the Sun sign, and the planet that rules the sign occupied by the Moon is called the Moon ruler.

These different rulings were established a long time ago. There are additional features and weightings given to the rulings, known as *exaltation*, *detriment* and *fall*. Each planet is exalted when it is in a particular sign from which it works well and with which there is a notable similarity, resulting in more significance being attributed to it in an interpretation. The exaltations are also listed in the table below:

Planet	Ruling in	Exalted in	Detrimental	Fall
☉ Sun	♌ Leo	Aries	Aquarius	Libra
☽ Moon	♋ Cancer	Taurus	Capricorn	Scorpio
☿ Mercury	♊ Gemini and Virgo	Virgo	Sagittarius	Pisces
♀ Venus	♉ Taurus and Libra	Pisces	Aries	Virgo
♂ Mars	♈ Aries	Capricorn	Libra	Cancer
♃ Jupiter	♐ Sagittarius	Cancer	Gemini	Capricorn
♄ Saturn	♑ Capricorn	Libra	Cancer	Aries
♅ Uranus	♒ Aquarius	Scorpio	Leo	Taurus
♆ Neptune	♓ Pisces	Leo	Virgo	Aquarius
♇ Pluto	♏ Scorpio	Virgo	Taurus	Pisces

The ruling planets and relationships

Opposing the ruling sign of the Zodiac, each planet also has a sign of detriment, from which it works less well. In this the planet is said to be weak or debilitated. The signs of detriment are listed in the table above. Finally, in this section comes the sign opposite to exaltation, which is called the fall sign. This is the sign of the Zodiac directly opposite to the sign of exaltation and, as with detriment, is where the planet is thought not to work as well. (See table above).

The Houses of the Chart

The astrological chart is divided into houses—in effect this is a way of subdividing the space around the Earth. There are numerous such systems, which have been devised over the years and which fall into three groups: the Equal House System; the Quadrant System; and a variation on these systems.

The *Equal House System* (*see* figure 4) is one of the oldest and after a period of disuse is now back in favour. The ecliptic is divided into twelve equal parts, and the houses are marked by great circles that meet at the poles of the ecliptic and start by going through the degree of the ecliptic ascending over the horizon, and then through every point 30 degrees farther around.

The main *Quadrant Systems* are called after the people who developed them, for example, Campanus, Regromontanus and Placidus, and appeared in the thirteenth, fourteenth and fifteenth centuries respectively. The system of Placidus was used almost exclusively until the early 1950s because it was the only system with published reference tables. It was, however, the only system that did not utilize great circles as the boundaries of the houses.

The final system, a variation, includes the system of Porphyry, which has its origins in antiquity. This is based on the Quadrant System, producing four unequal divisions that are then equally divided into three.

The Equal House System is probably the simplest to use, and in it each house has a certain relevance or significance,

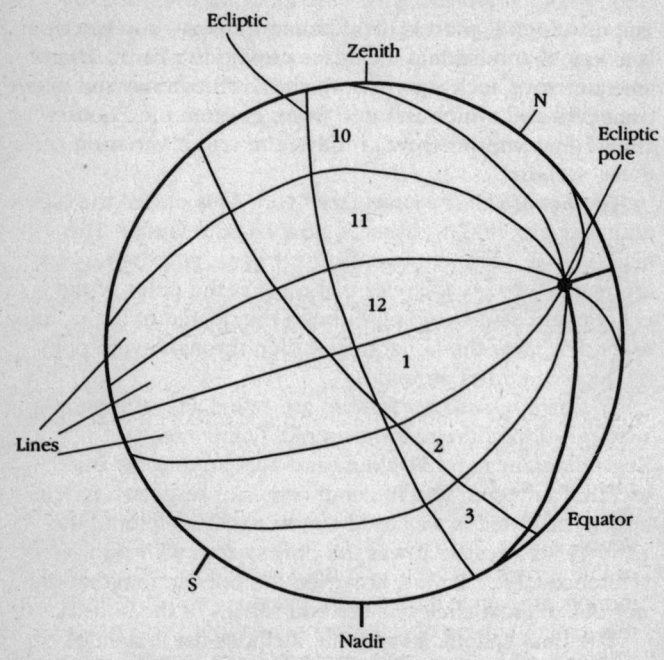

Figure 4: The Equal House System

affecting a particular aspect of life. The first six houses are concerned with a personal application while the last six apply more to one's dealings with other people and matters outside the home and family. There follows an expanded though not comprehensive description of each house, stipulating the association of house with sign and planet and the resulting meanings. In this context, the planets stand for the provision of an impetus; the signs show how and where that impetus or motivation is to be used; and the houses indicate in which aspect of life the result will be seen.

The Houses

The First House
This house is associated with Aries and the planet Mars, and because it includes the ascendant, or rising sign, is the most important house of the birth chart. This house refers to the person, which may include such factors as physical characteristics, nature, health, ego and so on. Planets within eight degrees of the ascendant will strongly affect all aspects of the person, including behaviour.

The Second House
The second house is associated with Taurus and the planet Venus, and is concerned with the possessions and feelings of the person. As such, this house reflects attitudes to money, and since money and love are intimately entwined, this aspect will be of relevance when interpreting a chart. The second house is also concerned with priorities and the growth of things.

The Third House
This is the house of Gemini and the planet Mercury, which not surprisingly means a concern for siblings and also

neighbours. Other matters of a local nature, such as schooling, local travel and everyday matters of business, fall under this house. A combination of these factors with mental attitude, which also falls into the third house, means that many decisions and patterns of behaviour, of fundamental importance, can be considered here. Decisions such as where to live and personal environment are typical examples.

All aspects of communication also fall within this house, including speech, letters, teaching, and so on. For anyone who is lost as to which direction to go in or what decision to take, a positive influence from the third house will help him or her to adjust mentally and escape the impasse.

The Fourth House
The sign of Cancer and the planet Moon are associated with the fourth house. The key concerns of this house are the home itself, home circumstances and the family, and caring for someone or something. The mother, or a mother figure, is a particularly strong feature of this house. The concept of the home and the protective enclosing also has analogy with the womb and the grave—thus, the beginning and end of life are also concerns.

The Fifth House
This house is very different from the fourth, and the association of Leo and the Sun makes it the house of pleasure and creativity. This includes all such aspects, whether they be related to art, authors, games, gambling, and other leisure pursuits. Moving into the more personal sphere, the fifth house also accounts for lovers and love affairs, probably on a superficial level rather than a lasting, deep relationship. The other personal manifestation of creativity, that of

producing children, and parents' feelings about children and procreation, fall under the rule of this house.

The Sixth House
The sixth house is the last that impinges upon the person and personal acts, behaviour and relationships. Its sign is Virgo and the planet is Mercury. This is a very functional house, referring as it does to work of a routine nature, health and similar matters. The work may be in the work place, hence it also relates to employers, or at home in the daily round of chores. The concern of health also includes diet, and this house will help to assess the need and timing for a change.

The Seventh House
The last six houses refer to the wider influences of one's life and to outward rather than inward application. Libra and the planet Venus are associated with the seventh house, and the fundamental concern is with relationships with others and partnerships. This house concerns commitment in partnership and can reflect the likely type of partner sought. It can also relate to the establishment of a business or the employment of new people, from the viewpoint of personal interaction. Because this house encompasses dealings with others, it can also include hostility and conflict.

The Eighth House
This house, the opposite of the second, is associated with Scorpio and Pluto, and refers to possessions gained through others, whether as gifts or legacies. In fact, all financial matters such as tax, joint money, insurance and corporate finances fall within this house. It is also the house of birth and death, or alternatively beginnings and endings. Deep

relationships, including those of a sexual nature, are dealt with, as are matters of the occult, and those of the afterlife.

The Ninth House
The ninth house, the house of Sagittarius and Jupiter, is from the opposite of the third, which is concerned with neighbours and matters local. The ninth focuses upon travel and mental activity but on a widespread basis, i.e. it covers travel (to foreign countries) and extensive study (as is further education), and also has been called the house of dreams. Longer-distance communication and matters such as the law and literature are covered by the ninth house. Indeed, all factors that potentially may increase one's experience or awareness are appropriate.

The Tenth House
The fourth house is concerned very much with matters of the home and family—a seemingly introspective vision. The tenth house is its opposite and looks outward to life in general, being concerned with hopes and ambitions and making one's way in life. It used to be called the house of the carer and the father, when perspectives and opportunities were more limited than today. As such this is the province of the long-term carer and also responsibility in the context of the delegation, both giving and receiving. This house is pertinent when career changes are considered, and is associated with Capricorn and Saturn.

The Eleventh House
The eleventh house is associated with Aquarius and Uranus. It is the house of acquaintances, social contacts and friends (but not close friends), and as such may encompass societies, clubs and similar groupings. It also provides an indica-

tion of whether a person looks favourably upon charitable causes and whether any activities in this direction are genuine or for the self—the house of social conscience in effect. It was called the house of hopes and wishes.

The Twelfth House

The twelfth house, associated with Pisces and Neptune, is linked with things that are hidden, self-sacrifice, psychic matters and also matters of an institutional nature. This last aspect may refer to hospitals or prisons, and as such may include the more serious illnesses. It also can shed light on problems of a psychological nature, reflected to some extent in its previous name—the house of sorrows.

As implied earlier, in The Signs of the Zodiac, the following chapter on the Sun signs, or the Sun through the signs, provides more information on personality, characteristics, associations and aspects of personal involvement and interaction.

The Sun Signs

sign: **ARIES** ♈
dates: 21 March to 20 April
origin and glyph: the ram's horns, which may be traced back to Egypt
ruling planet and groupings: Mars; masculine, cardinal and fire
typical traits: Arians have several noticeable characteristics, such as courage, seemingly boundless energy, enthusiasm, initiative and enterprise, and a desire for adventure and travel. This means that when faced with a particular challenge, there is a tendency to rush in without heeding the consequences, and this can often cause problems. This impulsiveness is, of course, one of their less appealing traits, and it may also be accompanied by selfishness. This manifests itself in the need to accomplish set tasks and reach planned goals, although they tend to have the beneficial quality of being able to concentrate on the primary aim by removing anything that is unnecessary and not of importance. Competitiveness is never far from the surface for an Arian, no matter what aspect of life is involved.
en famille: in personal relationships, Arians can be very passionate, and Aries men look for a strong partner. Arian women are equally demanding and often prefer a career to being at home, although the two can be combined. Providing there are no adverse influences

elsewhere on a person's chart, Arians are faithful but there are those who are continually moving on to new relationships and challenges.

Children of this sign tend to show the typical traits of liveliness and enthusiasm, but because there is always the underlying impatience, a child may soon lose interest and be looking for something new. Performance at school may be chequered because of this trait. However, should such a child lose his or her place or standing, his or her natural competitiveness and wish to lead usually reassert themselves, and lost ground is regained and held.

As parents Arians are, not unexpectedly, energetic and in the main will encourage their children in a variety of activities. It is all too easy, however, for the ebullience of the parent to overshadow the wishes of the child, and that can easily result in discord.

business: to satisfy the Arian character, an occupation ought to be challenging, with goals to aim for and with the opportunity to lead. Boring, routine jobs would not satisfy, but if that were the outcome then other activities would have to compensate. Large organizations with some freedom and a defined career structure, such as teaching, the police or the civil service, would be appropriate.

wider aspects: in their other pursuits, Arians import their eager approach, which in certain circumstances can be positively damaging, for example, knocks and bruises in the early years.

associations: colour—red; flowers—thistle, honeysuckle; gemstone—diamond; trees—thorn-bearing varieties; food—traditional rather than exotic.

sign: **TAURUS ♉**
dates: 21 April to 21 May
origin and glyph: the bull's head, which has links with early civilizations in Egypt.
ruling planet and groupings: Venus; feminine, fixed and earth.
typical traits: Taureans rely upon stability and security, both in an emotional and financial context, but granted this they can be extremely reliable, patient and tenacious. They tend to be persistent, methodical and to see things through to the end, and this can be reflected in their steady progress through life, including their career. Their lack of flexibility can often lead to resistance to change, even when it is for the better. However, when facing the challenge, they usually cope better than most. Taureans are practical people who dislike waste, and they tend to have high standards.
en famille: a good partnership is important to Taureans, and this means a happy harmonious partnership. Their need to put down roots and build can render them very good at making a home, as does the practical side of their character. They usually make good husbands and wives, and parents, but they may make the mistake of getting stuck in a rut. One of the faults of Taureans is jealousy and possessiveness, which can often be applied to a partner.

Having established a good home, Taureans will probably consider children to be very important, and the parents will strive to make their children happy. Babies and toddlers can be slow to reach the obvious milestones such as walking, but in later childhood things need to be learnt only once. Discipline is important because Taureans are essentially traditional and look for rules and guidance.

business: although Taureans do not like taking risks, they are ambitious. However, they are more likely to stay with a job than to chop and change, and will quite possibly remain in uninteresting employment because the income is well nigh guaranteed. Sure handling of money and financial affairs comes easily to Taureans, and many find careers in the financial sector.

wider aspects: routine is vital, and change or uncertainty makes them uncomfortable. They enjoy leisure pursuits but must guard against becoming too lazy.

associations: colours—pale shades, especially blue, pink and green; flowers—rose, poppy and foxglove; gemstone—emerald; trees—apple, pear, ash; food—generally like their food.

sign: **GEMINI** ♊

dates: 22 May to 21 June

origin and glyph: two children, from Castor and Pollux of Classical mythology, which are bright stars.

ruling planet and groupings: Mercury; masculine, mutable and air.

typical traits: these include such characteristics as liveliness, versatility and intelligence, but these are tempered to some degree by a nervous energy and a certain inconsistency at times. They are logical, ordered and very quick of mind, seeking variety in their lives, both at home and in their work. They tend to be good communicators but at times let their desire to communicate dominate all else. They can take in information very quickly if they are concentrating enough, but run the risk of knowing a little about a lot rather than grasping one topic in great depth. This is not necessarily a bad thing, of course.

en famille*:* the Geminian curiosity and versatility render relationships a little more prone than most to disruption or diversion. However, partnerships can last, particularly if the husband/wife finds an interesting companion with whom he or she can interact intellectually. Gemini women often marry men who can deal with domestic chores, as such women have no love of housework.

As parents, they can be lively and creative but sometimes over-critical. It is not uncommon for Geminians to make poor parents because they can be too impatient, too heavily involved in their own careers and over-competitive, seeking reflected glory in their children's achievements.

Gemini children are likely to talk and walk relatively early, and it will be necessary to keep them well occupied. It is often advisable to encourage them to finish anything they have started, to ensure numerous tasks are not left in various stages of completion. Because Geminians can also be quite cunning, and although they may be very able at school, they can often put their own thoughts before hard facts.

business*:* Geminians are very good when dealing with money and can, therefore, be admirably suited to banking or accountancy. As might be expected, the ability to communicate and the lively personality mean they may also fit well into employment in some aspect of the media or advertising. The pitfalls inevitably are that attention to detail may be lacking and that there must be variety. Conversely, they handle pressure well and are good at handling several tasks at once.

wider aspects: change and variety remain of paramount importance, whether in leisure pursuits or retirement. Individualism will dominate over group activities, which may become routine.

associations: colour—yellow, although most are liked; flowers—lavender, lily of the valley; gemstone—agate; trees—any tree producing nuts; food—salads and fruit, fish.

sign: CANCER ⊕
dates: 22 June to 22 July
origin and glyph: the glyph represents the breasts; Cancer probably came from ancient Babylon.
ruling planet and groupings: Moon; feminine, cardinal and water.
typical traits: the protective nature of the Cancerian is the overriding aspect of the character, but it is tempered by a stubborn and often moody streak. Although they tend of be the worrying type, Cancerians have a remarkably good intuition, and their instinctive reactions and decisions can usually be relied upon. There is a changeability about Cancerians that manifests itself in several ways. They can rapidly adapt to pick up information, habits, etc, from others. It also means that they can be touchy and, like the crab, may be hiding a soft, easily hurt person beneath a seemingly hard shell.
en famille: the caring nature of Cancerians makes them excellent at building a home and good at forming long-lasting partnerships. In general Cancerians like to look back in preference to forwards and commonly stay in the same house for a long period of time. A slightly negative aspect is that their protective nature can

become excessive and turn into clinging, and they may be touchy and occasionally snap for no apparent reason.

The sensitive almost retiring aspect of the character can be seen quite early in life, and this may continue to the point that they become very shy at school; they may hide behind a shell. It is commonly the case that Cancerians will eye new social contacts somewhat warily, keeping them at arm's length. However, when they get to know each other better, firm friendships can develop.

Cancerians usually like their extended family within a reasonably short distance and are keen to help anyone who may need their support.

business: Cancerians can turn their hand to most things, and their careful, intuitive approach can make them successful. They tend to work well with people and often adopt the role of mediator, where diplomacy is required. The caring professions (for example, medicine) are obviously well matched to the Cancer character, but teaching may also be suitable. Although business may prosper under a Cancerian, there is often a tendency, even a fear, to change, which may show itself as inflexibility.

wider aspects: Cancerians are extremely sensitive, and while outwardly they appear charming and friendly, they can be temperamental and subject to wide mood swings. In general they love change, and while travel appeals, home has the greatest attraction.

associations: colour—silver and pastel shades; flowers—white flowers, especially the rose, lily; gemstone—pearl; trees—none in particular; food—dairy foods and fish.

sign: LEO ♌
dates: 23 July to 23 August
origin and glyph: it probably originated in ancient Egypt, from the constellation; the glyph resembles the lion's tail.
ruling planet and groupings: Sun; masculine, fixed, fire.
typical traits: Leos tend to be generous, creative and yet proud individuals who nevertheless need to keep a tight rein on themselves to avoid becoming overbearing. The creative nature needs to find an outlet in whatever guise, and it is common for Leos to become organizers, with confidence and energy, although beneath that they may be rather nervous. The possible risk is that Leos may end up taking over and feel they always know best, so they must learn to listen to the views of other people. They can also display a temper, if only briefly, and are prone to panic if things go badly wrong. However, they generally regain control of the situation quickly. Their impatience and tendency to go over the top are countered by the abundance of their positive qualities.
en famille: to their partners Leos will be affectionate, but their strong will and urge to lead can make them rather domineering. However, they can be very sensitive, and criticism can cut deeply. As parents, Leos understand and encourage their children and will do anything to ensure they are not unhappy. However, they are not over-compliant and often associate with traditional values when it comes to behaviour and education.

Leo children tend to have an outgoing and bright personality, but they must not be allowed to be bossy towards other children, nor must their stubborn streak be allowed to develop. However, any criticism must be levelled in such a way as not to dent the rather fragile Leo self-confidence.

business: whatever their occupation or position, Leo individuals will work hard, in part because they are happier when they have people working for them. For many, luxury or glamour will appeal, and if they can achieve this through their employment then so much the better. As such, they may turn to acting, sport or working in the jewellery trade. They will often go for highly paid jobs, which they equate with status, but, equally, they make good employers, expecting the best of their employees but generous in return.

wider aspects: the Leonian is better leading rather than following and excels where generalities rather than attention to detail are accepted.

associations: colour—gold and scarlet; flowers—marigold, sunflower; gemstone—ruby; trees—citrus, walnut, olive; food—honey and cereals, most meats and rice.

sign: **VIRGO** ♍
dates: 24 August to 22 September
origin and glyph: the Egyptian goddess of grain (Nidaba) was probably the origin, and in old pictures the Virgin is shown bearing an ear of corn and holding a child; the glyph is the female genitalia.
ruling planet and groupings: Mercury; feminine, mutable and earth.
typical traits: Virgoans are traditionally shy and modest, hard-working and practical and yet, perhaps, rather dull. They have a well-developed tendency to criticize both themselves and others, and often allow this to go too far. If a positive tenor is applied to Virgoan traits, it results in

someone who works hard, is sensible and intelligent, and very good at detailed tasks.

Being essentially a worker, Virgoans are not interested in taking the lead but more in completing a task to the best of their ability. There is a likelihood that Virgoans will be worriers, and often they worry about nothing at all, which can be misconstrued or counterproductive. However, their own positive qualities are the best tools to deal with such problems.

en famille: Virgoans are very loyal in relationships and fond of their family, although this love may not manifest itself openly but rather in private. They may be self-effacing or even devalue themselves by feeling unworthy. A more common fault would be to over-criticize, but in the main they are caring, sound partners.

Children like to be kept occupied and at school will be neat, tidy and helpful. Their natural shyness may make them seem aloof, but if they can build up their self-confidence this will help them to keep worry at bay.

A great deal of time and attention will be paid to the home to keep it nice, but care should be exercised so that standards are not kept too high.

business: as already mentioned, Virgoans are not particularly ambitious and therefore are happier when supervised at work. If attention to detail is required then they are very capable and proficient in problem-solving or working in science or medicine. Although they like to be appreciated, they are happier working as a member of a team. They have an incisive style, useful in the media and the teaching profession.

wider aspects: there is a desire for purity, perfection and happiness, which, provided that their self-esteem is strong enough, is attainable through application of their own qualities.

associations: colour—grey, green, brown; flowers—bright small flowers, e.g. buttercup; gemstone—sardonyx (a white/brown banded variety of onyx); trees—nut producing varieties; food—root vegetables.

sign: LIBRA ♎

dates: 23 September to 23 October

origin and glyph: The element of the scales may have several origins, possibly from their use in weighing harvests; the glyph is similar to a yoke.

ruling planet and groupings: Venus; masculine, cardinal and air.

typical traits: Librans are true to their origin—they are always trying to achieve a balance, whether between views, negotiating parties, or in their own environment. In many instances, because they prefer not to take one side or the other, they sit in the middle, and this indecision can be their greatest fault. Turned to positive effect, by combining their desire to balance with their undoubted charm, Librans make fine 'diplomats' and can often settle an argument to everyone's satisfaction. They are also easy-going and like quiet surroundings at home or work, but although they may appear vulnerable, they are in fact quite tough and ensure that they follow their own plans.

en famille: in relationships with a partner, Librans can be complete romantics and regard this relationship as very important, so much so that even the Libran indecisiveness can be overcome for a time. They tend to fit well into the domestic scene, being quite capable of organising the household with their usual equable approach to all things, including money.

Librans make kind parents, although they must ensure that they are strong-willed and insist upon children doing as they are told. The Libran indecision might irritate some children, and every effort should be made to answer a child's queries. Children with this Sun sign tend to be charming and affable, and are often popular at school. Indecision and laziness should be identified and wherever possible overcome.

business: as mentioned, the tact and evenhandedness of Librans make them ideal as diplomats, in public relations, or any profession requiring these qualities. Their appreciation of art and beauty lends itself to a career in the arts or literature, and the fashion, beauty and related professions are all possibilities. Although they like to work with other people, especially those of a like mind, they are sufficiently ambitious to reach for the top, although any isolation that this might produce would be unwelcome.

wider aspects: Librans work well anywhere where there are pleasant surroundings that are well ordered.

associations: colour—blues and pinks; flowers—bluebells, large roses; gemstone—sapphire; trees—ash, apple; food—cereals, most fruits and spices.

sign: SCORPIO ♏
dates: 24 October to 22 November
origin and glyph: the origin of the scorpion is unknown, although it appears in numerous guises in ancient history. The glyph symbolizes a serpent's coil and is linked with the male genitalia.

ruling planet and groupings: Pluto; feminine, fixed and water.

typical traits: Scorpios can show rather a mix of behaviour and character, on the one hand being very determined and strong-willed, and on the other being obsessive, awkward and arrogant. Once committed to something, whether a person or an ideal, they will be very faithful, although they are susceptible to being melodramatic, and when emotions become involved logic suffers. They are usually energetic, wanting the most out of life, whether at work or play, and will not relinquish their goal easily. Although they are perfectly capable of sacrificing others, they do hold on to what is right and will exhibit a strong sense of fair play and reason.

en famille: the Scorpio's desire to stay with a relationship holds good for partnerships, although their energy may need to be channelled if it is not to prove disruptive. They prefer people who are equally strong-willed but, despite outward appearances, may themselves be weaker than they look. They are certainly prone to depression, from which they find it hard to emerge, and this may contribute to the apparent extremes in marriage—some are very good, others less so.

As parents they will do their utmost for their offspring, but they can push a little too much and should consciously develop a balanced approach to parenthood, allowing their children some freedom.

Some children are often very affectionate but equally prone to sudden tempers. They should be helped to talk over problems to avoid depressed silences, and their emotional energies should be diverted into productive occupations.

business: when running a business, a Scorpio will work to his very limit to help ensure success and, to a certain extent, they welcome challenges and problems. They can employ charm when necessary but can also be hard and demanding at times. They also like financial security and are willing to work for it. Scorpios are well suited to being in the medical profession or in a profession where analysis and research are required.

wider aspects: the character of a Scorpio is built up of a fine balance of attributes, which, in a positive sense, can yield a tremendous achiever but conversely may produce someone riven with jealousy.

associations: colours—deep red; flowers—dark red flowers such as geraniums; gemstone—opal; trees—thorn-bearing varieties; food—foods with strong flavours.

sign: SAGITTARIUS ♐

dates: 23 November to 21 December

origin and glyph: the origin is unknown, but the glyph, represents the arrow of the Centaur.

ruling planet and groupings: Jupiter, masculine, mutable and fire.

typical traits: Sagittarians are essentially gregarious, friendly and enthusiastic, with a desire to achieve all goals that are set. They are rarely beset by depression, but their inborn enthusiasm can sometimes take them too far, and they may take risks. Although they are versatile and intelligent, their desire to jump from the task in hand to the next in planning may result in some tasks being unfinished. In excess their good qualities can become a nuisance, leading to tactless, hurtful comments (without the intent to hurt) and jokes that go a little too far.

en famille: freedom is important to Sagittarians, so much so that it may inhibit long-standing relationships. After settling down, however, they are good in the family context, and their enthusiasm can help lift boredom or depression. Most Sagittarians will enjoy a friendship or partnership more if they are given a loose rein to enable them to do what they want. Often their ultimate goal is not materialistic but more spiritual.

As parents, this approach to life means that they encourage their children to be outgoing, and this is fine providing a child is not nervous or shy. The natural enthusiasm of Sagittarian children should be guided to productive ends, and their instinctive dislike of rules should be dealt with diplomatically if they are to reason. There is considerable potential in the child who has a gentle guiding hand upon him or her.

business: as already mentioned, Sagittarians are not interested primarily in material gain and because they are particularly interested in education and travel, that is where money may be spent. Work of a varied nature is preferred, but care should be taken to make sure details are not omitted in the race to move on to something new. There is a natural desire to help others, which may manifest itself in a career in teaching, counselling, lecturing, the Church, law, and even publishing.

wider aspects: when both mind and body have a certain degree of freedom, Sagittarians are at their best and will then employ their versatility and intellectual strengths to the full.

associations: colours—purple, deep blue; flowers—carnations; gemstone—topaz; trees—oak, ash, and birch;

food—good food is enjoyed but caution must be employed. Specifically currants and the onion family.

sign: **CAPRICORN** ♑
dates: 22 December to 20 January
origin and glyph: it may have originated with a mythical sea-goat from ancient Babylon. The glyph, is said to represent a goat's head and a fish's tail.
ruling planet and groupings: Saturn, feminine, cardinal and earth.
typical traits: it is said that there are two types of Capricornian, one of which has greater and higher hopes of life. In general, they are patient and practical and can be very shy, preferring to stay in the background rather than be in the spotlight. Even though they may be retiring, they are strong-willed and can stand up for themselves. Capricornians often have a reputation for being mean, and for being ambitious and rather hard people. A mean streak may often be directed at the self, and ambition, if tempered with realism and humour, can be a positive trait. It is usually the case that the character is enhanced by other elements of the chart to produce a warmer personality.
en famille: Capricornians make good partners, although they may come late to marriage to ensure a career has been established and that the correct choice is being made. Once set up, they are likely to be happy and to provide well, if economically, for the family. This aspect of caring can extend well outside the immediate family, and although there may be a lack of confidence, a Capricorn subject will not allow him or herself to be pushed around.

As parents, they are serious but sometimes can be too strict. However, they encourage their children and will make sacrifices elsewhere to assist their child's progress.

Capricorn children may be a little slow to develop but usually come into their own eventually. They are very loyal and benefit from a secure background, which offers discipline, but at the same time they should be helped to build up their self-confidence.

business: although they make very good back-room people, Capricornians can also do well leading from the front and in their own businesses. Many have an affinity for scientific work and can pay attention to detail when necessary. They are good when working with people, although they tend to have rather an isolationist attitude, taking advice only grudgingly. One might well find them in local government, finance, publishing, building or politics.

wider aspects: those with Capricorn as their Sun sign are generally happy alone in leisure pursuits and therefore enjoy music, reading, etc.

associations: colour—dark colours; flowers—pansy, ivy; gemstone—amethyst; trees—pine, willow; food—starchy foods, meat.

sign: **AQUARIUS** ≈
dates: 21 January to 18 February
origin and glyph: there are several links with the water carrier, and the glyph clearly resembles water waves, although the similarity to serpents has also been noticed.
ruling planet and groupings: Uranus; masculine, fixed and air.
typical traits: Aquarians are renowned for their independ-

ence and the fact that they like to operate according to their own rules. This can lead to them becoming very stubborn, which should be overcome, but they can be inspiring because they do not easily lose hope. Aquarians are friendly, although they may not be totally reliable when circumstances become difficult, and highly creative in terms of ideas. However, they are not necessarily sufficiently practical to see through the ideas. Overall, they may be a little perverse or paradoxical, but beneath it all is a gregariousness and a real wish to help.

en famille: because of their independence, Aquarians may find it difficult to establish an emotional tie. However, providing they find the right type, who is not weak but capable and sensible, personal relationships can be very successful. They are usually totally faithful.

With children, they are supportive but may find it difficult to cope with emotional problems. Children may be a little unconventional, and some school environments may not be conducive to the full development of their potential. Parents of Aquarian children should be aware of this. On the positive side, children will be originators, naturally friendly, and show the Aquarian traits of creativity and an affinity for science. The natural friendliness should not, however, be allowed to develop into a trust of anyone, particularly strangers.

business: not surprisingly, Aquarians like the freedom to do whatever they want, and they tend not to heed anyone who tries to boss them around. They are highly inventive and are generally good with any subject of a technical nature. They are also highly competent at practicalities. This makes for a considerable range of occupations, and Aquarians often turn their hand to science, communications, teaching, social work and general administration.

wider aspects: Aquarians are by their very nature a little out on a limb and unconventional, but their very positive qualities make this an interesting Sun sign.

associations: colour—electric blue; flowers—orchid; gemstone—aquamarine; trees—fruit trees; food—a light diet suits best, including fruits.

sign: **PISCES** ♓

dates: 19 February to 20 March

origin and glyph: there are numerous links between the two fishes and various deities from history, including Jesus Christ. The glyph represents two fish, linked, but also refers to the physical and spiritual side of the person.

ruling planet and groupings: Neptune; feminine, mutable and water.

typical traits: the Piscean person is really quite sensitive but above all is a highly sympathetic and caring person who invariably puts other people first, especially the family. They have great intuition and are good at understanding the needs of other people and make very good, kind friends. Sometimes they can take their idealistic and self-effacing stance too far, resulting in an unwillingness to face decisions, and sometimes they will rely on other, stronger, characters to lead for them. They are usually always tactful but should beware that helping others and becoming involved emotionally is not always a good thing.

en famille: in partnerships, Pisceans can be a little difficult to cope with, but with the right partner will help to build a welcoming home. They like visitors and to visit others, and their self-sacrificing attitude means that they will usually go a little bit further to make people happy, or an occasion just right. It is important that their lack of strong will is not exploited by a stronger character.

Pisceans love children and make very good parents providing they are not too 'soft'. They do have an inner strength, and can be very tough and resourceful if the occasion demands it and when they rise to the challenge. Children often take second place to others and may need some help with their self-confidence. However, they can be very good in science and with parental encouragement can be good achievers.

business: it is not surprising, with their caring instincts, that Pisceans make good teachers and members of the health and related professions. They tend not to be particularly ambitious but can have extremely good business minds. Success is usually more likely if they have a supportive business partner. Other professions that often attract Pisceans include acting, the ministry, and anything linked with the sea.

wider aspects: Pisceans have to be careful that in helping and caring for others they tend to ignore their own pursuits or problems.

associations: colour—sea green; flowers—water lily; gemstone—moonstone; trees—willow; food—excesses should be avoided, salad foods are very suitable.

The Chart

All the foregoing is background information that helps in the interpretation of a birth chart or horoscope. A typical blank chart is shown below. The solid central line represents the horizon and the numbered segments are the houses, as described previously. On this chart are plotted the positions of the Sun, Moon and planets.

To begin with, the following information about the subject is required:

- the date of birth
- the time of birth and whether it was British Summer Time or not
- the place of birth and the appropriate latitude and longitude

From this information, the position of the ascendant and midheaven can be plotted, followed by the planets' positions. As each planet is placed on the chart there will be certain angular positions developed between them, and when these form specific angles they are called *aspects*. These aspects have considerable influence on the chart and therefore on its subject.

In addition to these factors, there are further interpretive factors, depending on the placing of the planets in the various signs and the positions of these same planet in one of the twelve houses.

There are numerous books that show how to construct

Figure 5: The Birth Chart

a chart and begin the quite complicated task of interpretation. There are also computer programs that make the task a little easier. There is not the space to develop this part of the subject here, although all the information provided does give an insight into the character of an individual and the interesting approach offered by astrology.